Praise for *Roads Taken*

"These are some of the author's best works. You can't help but identify with his voice as he explores everyday things, life and feelings. Some poems sensuous, but sweet, others romantic, childlike, patriotic or thought provoking. Everyone will enjoy and share in these thoughts and experiences, ultimately believing in happiness and true love."

— Ann T. Scott, MA English, University of Michigan

"The poems within allowed me to see into the author's character and life experience. Honest, straightforward reflections of feelings, loss and love. Richness in each turn of the page."

— Michael G. Pacyga, musician, songwriter

"*Roads Taken* is a really enjoyable book, and easy reading, of a man in love. A very feel-good book, making you, the reader, think back about earlier days."

— Barbara Lynn Thomas, education registered nurse

"Mr. Carwile provides a glimpse into his life's journey, through a childhood steeped in playful memories, to his middle years of questioning the meaning of life and death, and reflecting on friendships. He comes full circle, through his poems of happiness, joy, despair and on again to happiness, continuing his life's journey. His poems are insightful and reflect his trials and tribulations as a boy growing up in the sixties, to a man in his sixties finding love again, seemingly for the first time. I found myself, as the character in his poems, relating to my life in his poetry."

— JoAnne Ragland, community relations administrator

ROADS TAKEN

That road I took,
so many years ago.
Coming back around
to its beginning.

ROADS TAKEN

By Tucker Carwile

BELLE ISLE BOOKS
www.belleislebooks.com

ISBN: 978-1-9399306-0-6
Library of Congress Control Number: 2015959452

Printed in the United States

Published by
BELLE ISLE BOOKS
www.belleislebooks.com

This book is dedicated to a special young lady who traveled many roads, taking journeys to many different places, but returning to our beginning and each other's arms.

Without her, this book would never have been completed. Thank you, RNB (Becky), for completing this journey with me.

ROADS FROM POCHIN PLACE

ROADS OF CONQUESTS

ROADS THROUGH THE MIDDLE AGES

ROADS FOR REFLECTION

ROADS TO HAPPINESS

ROADS FROM POCHIN PLACE

Dreams Seem Made

Remembering times forgotten,
of things not yet discovered.

Dreams dashed and ruined
and ages yet to come.
Our dreams seem made of thoughts,
not yet molded into reality.

A wisp of smoke,
never forming a flame.

Mother

You catch the brunt
of our emotions.
Seeing us when we are angry,
punishing us when we do wrong.
The one with whom we share
our quietness of secrets.

Whenever you cry
or seem tired,
we belittle you,
finding your weaknesses.

Little do we know much stronger
people would have yielded.

Slow to anger, but quicker
to forgive.
You gave your every moment,
for those trying times,
to stand beside us.

So remember,
even though we sometimes
forget,
we love you from within.

Father

How I remember those days.
You being strong and sure,
barking commands, and me
jumping at your every word.

I feared you,
but also respected your judgment.
Giving the right
direction,
always leading.

You gave to your friends,
never having enough time for
family.
But you see I never hated you,
for I loved you.

Now that you are sick and weak
leaving us leaderless and confused,
I still admire you
and will always protect you.

Playing in the Yard

As a child,
playing soldiers
bought with my money
at the "Five and Dime."

Heroes dressed in green,
brown as the enemy.

Many battles were fought
in my yard,
many victories achieved,
in such a short period of time
on a Saturday afternoon.

Simple Days

Those simple days,
when grass was green,
and the sky blue.

Life was like a fairy tale.
Good guys wore
white hats,
it only rained on weekdays
and true adventures were
found in Marvel Comics.

You were my
Mark Twain
and I was the issue
continued next month.

Battle Scars of Youth

Bicycles ridden,
no helmet or pads.
Skateboards,
with metal wheels,
boards homemade.

Scars were badges of
my youth.
Learning not how many
I collected,
but what not to do
next time.

Circus

The circus came
to town today.

Old lumbering elephants,
slowly moving down
Main Street.
Followed by creaking wagons,
filled with aged
lions,
tigers
and unicorns.

And giraffes, following to the rear,
bowing their massive heads,
under blinking lights.

I remember the
circus,
the mystical excitement
brought to me,
in my youth.

Quality of Life

The big top is
rising high.
Crews
pounding stakes, and
elephants pulling ropes
hooked to heavy canvas.

Excitement building, as
each performer, scurries
to complete their assigned
task.

And me, running home,
gathering my change
to make general admission.

I miss that
"Big Top";
a quality of life,
lost so many
years ago.

Friend

There was a time
when I had a friend.
We were close,
our minds being knitted
as one.

One day they left,
going their way
and I another.

I was young and had thought
the world had come
to the bitterest
of ends.

I trusted no one
and fell into myself–
until I found you.

Old House

Entering into your
hallowed halls.
The creaking floors,
hand-plastered walls.

The stories you could
tell,
from youth to aged.
Of lovers spats,
and warm embraces.

Of new life,
and ending death.
Families grown but
now have gone.

With only you
to keep the
diary.

Changes

Shall I tell you
about tomorrow,
those changes that will
never be.

People we meet today,
will be strangers tomorrow.
Things shared
as we grow,
are never those
things of tomorrow.

Treehouse

We built a treehouse
once,
my best friend
and I.

Our parents told us
"not too high,"
they didn't want
any broken bones.

Drawing plans and
gathering spare lumber,
we started on a
Saturday.

Working
in the summer heat,
bandaged thumbs
and scrapes from
rusty saws,
we finally moved in.

Sitting inside
our "grand castle," we
planned the
conquest of the world.

Ventilation

We spent many
a day
and night
in our treehouse.

Lying in our sleeping bags,
staring at the moon
through spaces in the roof;
we called it
ventilation.

Afternoon Storm

After the rain,
sun setting through
broken clouds.
Colors of orange, green hues
with gray,
appear setting
piecemeal.

First the top,
then exposing the center,
and lastly God's
blue ocean.

The beauty of the day,
exposed for all
to see.
No painter's canvas
can match
God's color palette.

Last Night's Dream

I met you in a dream last
night.
We sat and talked
as learned people do;
speaking of things
above my mind.

And when we were
through,
we hugged
and got married.

Now we watch the
planes,
take off and land
in our backyard.

Beach Time

How good you taste,
the salt from the sea
mixed with your body;
it seems the perfect match.

You, with your bronze skin,
make me jealous
of the time you spend
with the sun. If I could have
that time
the beach takes you from me,
would I ever be alone.

Religion

How often man
goes to war,
for God and religion.
Genocide,
in the name of the father.

Thou shalt not kill,
but okay for the faith.
How many deaths,
to bring peace to
a nation.

I wonder how God feels about
all this,
or is religion
just a made-up word.

And God loves us all.

My Future

While I sit here wondering
what,
if any,
my future will be.
I look deep into myself
and see a boy,
trying to become a man.

ROADS OF CONQUESTS

Once Dreamt

I once dreamt of
flying around the world,
invulnerable to pain.
Able to see deceit and wrongdoing
with a single glance.

I still have those dreams,
but now keep them
to myself.

I have no thoughts of grandeur,
or saving the world.
Reality and pain
have seared their
marks into me.

Voting

Today we voted on a forum
how much we really care.
Me, myself and I
elected you as the nicest
person we know.

I know the election
was fair.
For you see,
I know the voters well—
a fair and impartial lot.

Being Alike

You see, you're a lot like me.
You worry when I frown and
boost my spirits when I'm down.
Worrying about the small things
that have already happened.

Maybe that is why we are attracted
to each other—
we both distrust the world
and its many false people.

Full Cycle

Moving in, meeting neighbors
for the first time.
Raising children,
watching them grow.

And as time passes,
faces disappearing.
Houses emptying,
as children grow and leave.

Then one day,
new faces appear.

Me,
much older,
now greeting younger families.

Has my neighborhood
run full cycle,
as we all must do.

Moving On

There comes a time
in life.
Looking around,
gone are the buildings
that stood
fifty years or more.

Shops shuttered,
once visited daily,
never to be enjoyed again.

iPads, iPhones and tablets,
where
paper and pen once used.

I understand now,
why living to 100
might be a bad thing.

Peace Treaty

Gathering on the lawn
today,
we set the rules.
Taking questions,
answering the best
I could.
There were those afraid
I'd finish
the job I started
many years ago.

"Why cut us down,
just because you built
too close";
"We did nothing wrong."
"And please stop
driving nails;
it hurts, you know."

By day's end,
the "treaty of trees"
had been signed.
They will be free to grow,
unless a storm
approaches.

Back-Door Neighbor

Every neighbor
needs
a back-door friend.

Someone to watch
over your family,
coming to your
aid with just a call.

Being there if trouble
enters your home.
But only long enough to
console, or
bring a casserole.

Those neighbors are dear,
never to be forgotten.
For they are the
life blood,
of our neighborhood.

End Thoughts

As darkness,
descends into night,
my mind rushes
from the day's
indecisions.

The stillness, broken by
the humming from
an aged refrigerator,
smoke rising from a
smoldering cigarette,
and songs streaming from a radio
too new to remember.

I wonder
what this time could have
been,
with you by my side.

Sunrise

Have you ever watched
a sunrise?
Light emerging from darkness,
sun filtering through clouds
or boiling from the ocean.

You are that light.
Warming me,
letting me see there is
nothing in the darkness
that will hurt me.

Whenever the sun rises,
I will think of you.
And when it sets at night,
I won't be afraid
knowing that tomorrow
I'll be with you.

Sorry

"I'm sorry" seems so poor a word
for ruining someone's day.
Even when spoken with the
eloquence of a senator,
or the innocence of a child.

The results always the same,
missed appointments,
broken dates,
plans that took weeks
to formulate.

"Sorry," so shallow a word,
with so many meanings.

Reading Words

Each word guarded,
as being spoken.
Reading many meanings,
looking under words
that have no bottom.

The wars must have
been hard.
Sparring, as only a fighter
could know.

It makes better sense
to watch flowers grow,
than think of hurtful words.

You see, all I'm saying is
"I like you."

Enough Time

Take from me the things I have,
share the time I have
to offer,
but nothing more.

If I could,
I would spend all
my time with you,
sharing each new experience.

Asking me to change
would destroy the me
you know.

You bring to me a peace and a joy
that can never be found
on any mountaintop.

Into Your Mind

Talk to me a while
before the night replaces the sun.
Tell me of things
which dreams are made,
and the darkness has
nothing to hide.

Lead me like a child,
into your mind.
And when you've taught me
your ways,
show me the moves
that made love
so famous a word.

Second Look

Lying here beside you,
I wonder what life
is about.

Another time and place,
or if peace
reigned at home,
would you have even looked twice.

Wordless

Should words be spoken today,
or just left unsaid.

A kiss, embrace,
or just a look,
says far more than
words.

Mechanical sometimes,
spoken out of text,
with no thought.

Look into my eyes,
and read a novel,
with no words being
spoken.

Drifting Apart

I'll be with you,
until I'm no longer needed.
A shoulder to touch,
a body to lie beside.

One day, and it will come,
we will drift apart.

Me a memory,
a past not forgotten,
and you a page in some
unwritten novel.

Forever

Who could think
within moments,
this quiet path will be
strewn with pain and death.
Waiting quietly for the enemy
to emerge.

Faces not seen and unknown,
they then appear.
Young, so young,
screaming and dying,
always coming.

Then I awake,
knowing that with tomorrow's eve,
they will be back again.

Lone Eagle

Soaring above the land
as though you rule the whole domain.
Majestic in stature,
noblest of all.

Your emblem has led armies to war,
and ruled countries at peace,
becoming the symbol of
greatness and power.
You have yielded to man's
every move,
sacrificing yourself for freedom.

All you ever wanted
was to be left alone.
To live your life in
lonely solitude with those
of your own.

Now you have become an endangered
species.
Ever slowly moving back
from man's progress.

Reason for Leaving

No more than a child,
so young and loving.
Not yet knowing of hate
and jealousy.

Your reason for leaving,
unclear.
Only that you passed
beyond that
last return.

Was life so terrible,
that death was the only solution?
Answering is pointless,
for these questions have
no meaning.

You came as a blessing and
there will always be a memory
of you.
Did life fail you,
or was it just not your time for living.

The Load

How often you
carried my thoughts,
reacting to my
every whim;
deeds thought
undoable.

Now lying
broken and crushed,
my thoughts cannot
move you.

It is me,
who will now carry the
load.

The mind and body,
forever separated.

Confused

That night so long
ago,
on the beach.
The night you
went away confused
and hurt.

Think not you were to
blame,
for I was afraid,
not knowing the moves
to make you happy.

Many a day has passed,
wishing I had been able
to practice,
before that special
evening.

ROADS THROUGH THE MIDDLE AGES

Time Passing

As with each tick of the clock,
time passes,
never being able to recover
those lost seconds.

Should we spend our time working,
or should we reflect on life?

If we work, then we have
gotten much closer to our goal.
But if we reflect,
could we not live the next
second better.

Yellow Tag

Little boy with your yellow tag,
are you coming home
or leaving?

Those tears in your eyes
mean something.
Is it one of happiness
or sadness?
Are you from a broken home,
traveling between parents.

I offered you a candy bar,
but you refused.
Taught never to accept gifts
from strangers.

When I boarded my flight,
you stayed behind
waiting for another.
I wanted to stay,
but knew you had someone
waiting at the other end
of your journey.

Good Is Enough

All I ever wanted was happiness,
is that so wrong?
Not ever being the best,
only good.

Why do people think
best is great.
It isn't, you know.

I judge my friends on
themselves.
Not how great
they want to become.

Friends Needed

A person never able to come
when needed.
Whose shoulder, available
per appointment,
days in advance.

Being so close,
but always so far.
Advising, after the fact,
when the crisis is
long forgotten.

Their importance somehow
escapes me.

Power

How strange that power corrupts
the pureness of hearts,
the closeness of friends.

There have been a few,
who survived,
but even on those it has
left its mark,
not always for the good.

Remember the path of
your life,
is not kept clear by
jewels nor gold,
but by those who will always
love you.

The Top

If by chance
you reach the top,
try looking back
at those untold bodies.
Heaped behind,
friends and
foes alike.
Remembering nothing
is forever.

Reach back a hand,
to build that bridge.
For it is loneliness at the top
that kills,
not your friends.

Ode to a Muffin

How caringly I mix
the batter.
Adding this and that,
just enough stirs
to thicken the mix.

Finally adding those
last few flavors.

Baking slowly,
watching each muffin rise
just right.
As a mother, nurturing her child.

Then removing when the tops
are lightly browned.

But before they have
cooled enough to eat,
one of the number
is missing.

Say Hello

I walked the streets today,
past rows of
shuttered people hiding
in their houses.

Those still asleep
or just afraid—
to pull their blinds
to meet the day,
or greet a stranger's
face.

Faces aren't bad,
you know,
just to say hello.

Worth Living

The reason, like life,
is never ending.
Always a surprise
around each and every
corner.

Some people come as they
often do,
without saying
hello or goodbye.

But for those
who have made their mark.
Does this make
life worth living?

Close Friend

I heard today,
my friend of thirty years
died in January;
this is August.

How could someone
so close,
so long ago, have left
without telling me
goodbye.

Frosty Days

Gazing through
my bedroom window,
ice formed from
the night's chill.
As though an artist's hand,
laboring for hours,
on each design.

And with the rising sun,
melting.
Joining its companions,
puddling
at the bottom of the pane.

Time at Peace

There must be time for peace,
writing down those things
that have been forgotten
through my workaday life.

I must reflect,
conforming my life that changes
from day to day.

If this time cannot be found,
my life can never be brought
into perspective
and I must wander through
time and space.

You never realize this lost time
until it is gone.
If you never take this time alone,
then how can you reflect
on the past and future?

Forgotten

Dying is a part
of living,
of being human.
That all things must
endure.

But being forgotten,
is a fear all too real.
Only
remembered as,
"What's his name"
or
"You know..."

Living your life,
raising a family and
making your footprint.
I'd like to be remembered
by my name, face and deeds,
not as,
"I remember him,
I went to high school with him."

Each a Person

Walking through a cemetery,
seeing names
and dates;
some so worn,
unable to be read.

Each a person
as you or I.
A life and purpose,
dreams and despairs.
Were they happy,
and was their life complete?

And, as I,
had they taken this walk through
the cemetery
a long time ago.

Traced Paper

Strolling through cemeteries,
paper and pencil
in hand.
Final farewells too weathered
to understand.

"Here lies Jesse
a Saint to us all,
he covered the miles
'til he got home."

Words written,
with no meaning today.
Those thoughts,
now forever lost.

I think my epithet will read
"He lived until he died."

Rain

Cold and wet
against my face,
washing away the pollen,
cleansing the air.

Praised by some,
cursed by others.
Falling when it wants,
not governed by man's
whims or wishes.

Its water, like life
cleanses my soul,
starting anew.

It should rain on everyone,
at least once a day.

Looking Back

Seeing the paths taken,
not always being right.
The stumbles and
the falls.
Mistakes aplenty,
enough to fill ten volumes.

But seeing the
past journeys
and the roads taken,
the end result
appears to be good.

So I feel at this time
a "mulligan"
will not be needed.

Yesterday Person

Yesterday lasts forever,
while today ends with the
setting sun ...

Tomorrow is for dreamers,
who never see the dawn.

I'm a yesterday person,
living with my thoughts
of tomorrow.
Knowing that tomorrow
never comes,
but somehow afraid of today.

My Birthday

You ask me what
I want for my
birthday.

Just your love
enveloping me
on cold winter nights.
Holding my hand,
walking on warm
summer days,
or sharing my umbrella in
stormy weather.

But let's make it simple,
just be with me
for the rest of my life.

No ribbons needed.

Valor

So young and innocent,
giving that last measure.
Asking questions only to yourself,
making that final journey
home—alone.

What was the last thought before
closing your eyes?
Was it one of disbelief,
thinking you could never die.
Or was it one of valor,
knowing you had done your duty.

Now, your name, etched across some
black marble stone
with so many others.
Above your head flies a flag,
and fresh flowers mark
your grave.

You leave your family
with a box of medals.
They, somehow, lack the
warmth of your flesh.

Middle Ages

In my middle ages,
love was a three-letter
word.
Conquest was the
objective,
let nothing stand
in my way.

And then I aged,
and the victories
seemed hollow,
nothing but pain
left behind.

Now as I age,
love has new
meaning and feeling,
kindness,
caring and you.

But these were the feelings
in the early years.

Maybe I should have
skipped the middle ages,
and passed
from early to late.

ROADS FOR REFLECTION

Making Waves

If time were measured in eons,
how short our lives would be,
nothing but a millisecond.
Can we make a wave in
such a short time,
would it be worth the sorrow
and hurt.

Like robots we live our lives
from decade to decade,
and before we realize,
"Rest in Peace."

If life was as simple as a poem,
how easy it would all be.

Icon

An Icon died
today.
Someone who
could wear the
theater mask and
bring tears with one,
and laughter
the other.

What demons made him
pass
that final mark,
as so many have done
but without the fanfare
of public outcry.

My Flag

I flew my flag today.
It showing signs of bare threads
and ruffled edges,
I knew it would soon need to be replaced.

We had been together for
so many years.
Through storms of ice and snow,
and sunny days with warm
spring breezes.

I wonder if friends,
like flags,
can be replaced when they
wear out.

Golden Oldies

There is something
to be said for,
listening to the
Golden Oldies.

Remembering places and times
so long ago.
Songs we cried to,
made love to.

But most of all,
songs that remind me
of the love
I have for you.

Leaving the Beach

I will leave the beach today,
after so many years.
Walking my last dune,
seeing the last
pounding surf.

How much you've
changed,
after all these years.

You, finding new
souls;
how many they've
become.

The solitude I seek,
shared by many,
my thoughts no longer
pure.

I leave now to explore
the person I am
becoming.

Meeting the Writer

I met the writer once.
A nice guy,
with blue eyes
and a faraway look
etched into his face.

He spoke of wanting
happiness,
love and understanding.

He tried for so long,
merging writings into
life,
but never the two
could be joined.

He said it took him sixty years,
before they
seemed as one.

He's happy now.

Watch Thingies

Those watch thingies
that tell you
how many steps
you take.

Are they calorie
counters,
or just lazy movements.
How many times,
you dreamt last night,
or did that even count.

What happened to the days
of walking
with someone special,
bringing just a smile.
Or waking in the arms
of the one
you love.

It costs nothing, you know,
and need not be ordered
through Amazon.

The meaning goes
much deeper.

Changing Beach

I remember the beach
of long ago.
Walking miles,
without sight
of sun worshippers.

We walked together,
hand in hand,
oblivious to the seagulls
keeping their watchful vigil.

Now that beach
is gone.
Filled with folks
with farmers' tans
and yelling kids.
Heavy with their
umbrellas,
towels
and coolers.

Blind As a Bat

I watch the sky
turn from blue to gray, not yet black.
Bats darting to and fro,
as if they could see
each insect
they will devour.

Stars starting to
twinkle,
I'm thankful for a day
complete.

And wonder how many
kisses and hugs
I can steal tomorrow.

Counter Culture

I watched a movie today,
from my generation;
free love,
drugs
and insanity.

My body never crossed
that counter culture,
but my mind
passed over a couple times.

My mind grew
from all of this,
but my body
stayed behind.

Even today my mind
makes cloud games,
and talks to the
ocean and trees,
while my body ages.

Porch Time

Sitting on my porch
watching walkers,
bicyclists, joggers;
old and young alike.

I see all types big and small;
designer outfits
or just jeans and tops.

Dragging their pets,
or being dragged.

Pounding pavement,
shedding those extra pounds.
It will only last until
the first cool breeze
that blows.

Then we all retreat inside to watch
"The Cooking Channel."

Reclaim

Sitting in my room,
watching the pendulum
of my clock moving,
marking the passing
of each second;
a part of my life
never to be reclaimed.

Ever moving forward
each second,
minute and hour;
without that thing
I require the most—you.

Saying Farewell

Goodbyes should be saved for funerals,
not for us.
We have marched too many miles,
sung songs of love, and
lay beneath the sun as one.

We've made our place together,
you becoming a part of me,
and I a part of you.

So if it's time to say farewell,
we'll hug and give a fond embrace,
and smile that everlasting smile.

And if by chance we meet again,
you'll look at me
and I at you.
And know how strong our love can last,
without a spoken word.

Bouncing

I climbed a tree today,
not too high
'cause I've heard,
old folks don't bounce.

Really Changing

While looking at these albums
of so long ago,
wondering why.
Pictures making us remember
how much
we've really changed.

The innocence,
never to be recaptured;
toy cars and
bikes with training wheels.

To see us then,
we could have lived
a million years.

Vacation

I signed up for that
6-day, 5-night stay
in June.

The weather not important,
having inside games
to play.
I entertained visitors
a number of times
a day.

Food not too bad,
the chef really tried.

And when it ended,
packing up to leave.
A stranger entered
extending his hand and said,
"Welcome to the
Zipper Club."

Images

After the last guest has gone,
the last plate cleaned
and returned to its shelf.

The house, is so quiet,
as though you'd never
been there.
As if forty years together
had been but a dream.

But listening, I still
hear your footsteps
quietly moving down
the hall.
Your image so clear
only to me.

We'll sit and talk tonight,
but only one voice will
be heard.

Battles

You've been to war
a thousand times,
in your mind.
Battle lines drawn,
readying for the fight,
but remembering the casualties.

The war will be won
if we stand
together.
But these battles
do sometimes cause pain.

Remember Me

A relative died,
and I attended
the service.

I knew her not,
but always the things
she did.

She seemed to have a look
of serenity;
not a look I ever saw her wear.

Calling the Shots

You hear them say at funerals,
completing their time on earth,
"They went to be with
their father,"
or the young ones,
"He loves little children,
and he needs them by his side."

I wonder if God really
needed that nine year old,
or that infant at birth.
The void and pain
that's left behind can cause
no one any good.

So I begin to think,
is God really calling
the shots?

Casket

When I die,
close the casket lid;
place plenty of
pictures around.

Some will come
because they're
family,
others will come
because they care.

And the bill collectors
will come just to make
sure I'm there.

Never Leaving

Ever wonder about
wandering souls.
Those never leaving,
waiting for what?

Religions say this
can never be true,
people testifying
they have left and
then returned.

Can a soul be around
once the body
has ended?

Me Time

When I'm confused
and exhausted,
I go to the farm.

Mounting my tractor,
engaging the blades.
No other thoughts,
not even
whether the lines
are straight, or grass
too high
or low.

It brings a
soothing to my mind.

For those four hours
I am at peace with myself,
and the world.

ROADS TO HAPPINESS

Second Meeting

Somehow feeling as
a young man courting.
Wondering what to say
or do.

What flowers do you like,
your favorite color,
the music,
is this the right band.

Thousands of thoughts,
each important as
the last.

The act of courting,
is something I never
thought would come again,
but with the right person...

Should I just be
the person I've become,
and you the person
you are;
filling in the blanks as we go.

To Becky

Was there a time,
I was looking,
without seeing.

So wrapped up in
my small world.
Passing by those
who really cared.

If only my eyes,
had not been cloudy.
That other road
would never have been
taken.

Two Lonely People

Two lonely people,
grasping at things that
will never be.
Hoping life will be kinder
this time around.

Wondering why love has
eluded them;
always found in someone else's eyes.
Reaching for that someone;
touching,
yet still so far away.

Can happiness be found
this time,
or is the carnage too great,
the scars too deep.

Hand in Hand

Take my hand,
hold it tightly.
For it has been
many years,
since last I walked
hand in hand,
with feeling.

How well we fit,
as a pair of well-worn gloves,
together a perfect match.

Thank You

Thank you for coming
full circle,
to finish this journey.

Thank you for
moving the clouds of confusion
that hung for so long.

Thank you, for
wanting to see this quest
completed,
without the thoughts
or doubts
that might have been.

But most of all
thank you for being you.

Not Yet Complete

As I bare my soul
to you.
Knowing me as no
other person has,
or ever will.

Am I not a person
as most,
no stronger or weaker.
Racked with mistakes
and misgivings,
always taking the roads
less cluttered.

I've decided
my decision is correct,
and my story
not yet complete.

Be mine in body and soul,
and if we stumble,
we'll be there, together,
to pick each other up.

A Little Longer

My desires,
so strong,
feelings of you
beneath my body,
living dreams
of days gone by.

But at this time,
our passion is
tempered by fear
of causing pain.

After such a long time,
waiting a little longer
is child's play.

Travel

Be gentle tonight,
take me to places,
where lovers go.

To plateaus yet to be
reached,
and valleys
never explored.

Show me colors,
yet to be mixed,
and dreams never
dreamt.

And when we return,
we will be
as one.

Invitation Only

Lie with me
a while.
We'll count the stars,
and plan our
home.

Building our castle in the sky
away from
those that doubt;
posting
"invitation only."

And while we sleep,
we'll dream and awaken
in each other's arms.

Young Lovers

How cruel the Gods of Love
can be.
Taking two lovers,
starting anew with life
and blocking them;
throwing confusion and fear
into their lives.

And after so many years,
bringing them back together.

What was their plan,
and did it do
any good.

Touching

Sitting beside you,
arm draped around
your shoulder
hand touching flesh.

I'm amazed
how soft your
skin feels.
Like the smoothness of
an angel's
would be.

Burden

Afraid to bring
to you.
To see you fall
into those depths,
into which
I myself have gone.

You must be saved
to carry on
our family history;
you alone our spokesman.

It's not I love you
less,
but more.
For you are my
sister.

This burden
was far too great for me.

Breakfast in Bed

Do you eat
pancakes in bed,
or has your
etiquette taught
you "no."

I think of what
makes you smile.
Spilling syrup
on your leg
and me licking
it clean.

Or do we sit
at the breakfast table,
with our coffee
and muffins.

Somehow, licking
syrup off your
leg seems best.

Teacher

You've taught me
to love, purely;
asking nothing in return,
the way we loved so many
years ago in our youth.

Your love,
bringing a calmness to my soul.
I cannot go back
to that person I was.

The person I want
to be today;
compassionate and loving,
wanting to share with those
who have nothing.

I need you,
leading me through
the wonders of life.

Starting Anew

So many years have passed,
shall we wait another
second,
knowing that time waits
for no man or woman.
Those lost years,
never to be recovered,
lost forever.

Starting anew can sometimes
be better.
And if life would
end today,
our reunion would have been
"the grand finale."

Come to Me

When ready,
come to me
without a word.
Soft feet, carrying you
above the floor.

Together we shall
merge into one,
throwing doubt into
the wind.

Questions already asked
and answered.
No more words
will be needed.

Innocent

To be so young
and innocent,
having seen such violence
of death and pain,
not seen by seasoned soldiers.
To know the final end,
eternity.

But moving forward,
stronger now always
guarded.

You will receive from me,
only love
and understanding.

Stay with me
and I will become
your shining knight,
protecting you
from those evil deeds.

Extra Time

How strange it
could be,
traveling back years,
possibly decades.
Warning those we cared
about,
of strokes, heart attacks.
Or not to be at that
location
on that date and time.

Would it be selfish
to gather that extra time,
and would we use it wisely.

Compare Notes

Write me a poem today,
not with your head,
but with your heart.

Tell me of love,
and hurt that has
made your life.

Lead me down paths,
started but
never completed.
And dreams yet to be
reached.

When you have finished,
we shall compare notes;
two hearts merged into one.

Hold On

For one
who has seen
such pain
and sorrow.

You bring out
such laughter in me
not seen for decades.

A touch so soft,
caressing,
so soothing
even to calm
the discord of
my life.

It has taken almost a
lifetime to find
you again,
and I will never
let you go.

Vows

To speak those vows,
spoken a hundred times before,
and many broken before
the end of day;
I refuse.

Instead, I will make you
a promise.
To watch over you,
and protect you
from harm.
Be there when needed,
but allowing you to grow
as the person you are today.

Giving you enough love,
to cover fifty years,
so long delayed.

And when our days end,
there will still be
enough love
for fifty more.

Journey

Hold onto my
hand,
for we are taking
that journey.

To faraway places,
created just for
you and me.

We will paint the
sky blue,
watch the sun set,
and the moon rise
as the rain falls.

And when we return,
we will leave
our room
to start our day.

Final Chapter

Seeing you smile,
with laughter.
How wonderful these
thoughts make me
feel.

I find myself laughing
out loud,
cracking those lines
forged by time.

The book that has been
written
is not my
final chapter.

8/2014

You ask me
if I need a ring;
it's not for me.

For I know my love
for you,
no ring will be needed.

But for all the
world to see...
that love can happen
to one like me.

Baring My Soul

Letting you see me,
as I am.
Baring my soul
as an open book.

Never let me get
tired of you,
or try to read you.

Open each morning
as God does
the sun,
and each night a
different star.

You know,
we can grow old together,
unless you
grow tired of me.

You Make Me Laugh

You make me laugh,
something so long
ago forgotten.

Tears streaming down my face,
not of sadness,
but of joy.
Awakening a person,
thought dying.

Like riding a
rainbow
to a golden valley,
once thought
destroyed.

Morning Coffee

I've never seen
you in the morning.
Glittering sunshine,
outlining your form
as you stir
to wake.

The smile, creasing your lips,
at the first words,
"I love you."

And me, with my
morning coffee,
can only stare
at our love.

No Agenda

I think of you
often.

Your smile,
like no others,
a laugh pure
and sweet.
A look that seems
to gaze into
my soul.

I think that is
why I love you—
there is no agenda.

Silly Boy

I want to see
that silly girl
again,
the one last night
who touched my heart.

Not the one who
reads meaning into
my off-color words.

Take me as I am,
a silly boy;
someone who still
believes in love.

When We're Apart

Hold me,
as though tomorrows
come no more.
Tell me
of happiness forgotten,
only to be recovered
by you.

Kiss away those fears
that enter
when we're apart.
Soothe those doubts
that plague my
every waking thought.

Your House

Entering your
house today,
sensing the aroma
of the past; hidden kisses,
and holding hands.

How well it has kept
our secrets, for
so long.

As I walk through
its rooms,
it asks me to stay.

It likes the games
we used to play.

Tribute

The uniform,
creased to perfection.
Shoes and buttons
polished to see
a reflection.

Speaking not a word,
eyes affixed.
As on a mission,
always counting those
twenty-one steps.

Giving respect to those
before them.
Giving honor to those
who served their
country well.

There are many
who have traveled this
road before,
and many more will follow.

But for this moment,
it is *you* they
are honoring.

My Muse

You bring a joy
to my being.
Head lying against
my chest,
your hands holding
my soul.

A joy I've longed for
all my life.
Seeming so natural;
as a period ends
a sentence,
a semi-colon starts
a thought.

Saying "I love you";
an understatement.
You are "My Muse,"
as I write
my poetry of life.

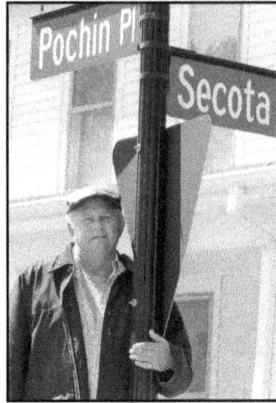

About the Author

Tucker Carwile was born and raised in the Hampton Roads area of Tidewater, Virginia, where he lives today. His youth was centered around the neighborhood and friends, sailing, bicycling, building treehouses, cutting grass each summer, playing football on Saturdays, and church on Sundays. This is where he first met Becky, who would later become his partner in life. After many years apart, they reunited, having taken different roads often filled with sorrow and sadness.

Taught in the principles of religion, Tucker learned early on that life can be much more complex, not as written in fairy tales. He has traveled extensively, exploring the beauty of nature and the tranquility of solitude. His biggest wonders have always been contemplating his choices in life and "what-ifs." Whether walking beaches, the streets of cities and towns, or camping in God's house beneath tall pines and mountains, Tucker has written down his thoughts and feelings about everyday life.

He started writing during college and received his Bachelor of Science degree from Christopher Newport College. This is where he also developed a love for teaching, but he took many entrepreneurial roads before he was able to return to his love of teaching and complete his journey.

Tucker published his first book of free verse, *Lone Sentinel*, in 2013. *Roads Taken* is his second collection, and he expects to complete a third collection in the future.